Fruits

by Grace Hansen

Abdo
PLANT ANATOMY
Kids

abdopublishing.com

Published by Abdo Kids, a division of ABDO, PO Box 398166, Minneapolis, Minnesota 55439.

Copyright © 2016 by Abdo Consulting Group, Inc. International copyrights reserved in all countries. No part of this book may be reproduced in any form without written permission from the publisher.

Printed in the United States of America, North Mankato, Minnesota.

102015

012016

 THIS BOOK CONTAINS RECYCLED MATERIALS

Photo Credits: iStock, Science Source, Shutterstock

Production Contributors: Teddy Borth, Jennie Forsberg, Grace Hansen

Design Contributors: Laura Mitchell, Dorothy Toth

Library of Congress Control Number: 2015942104

Cataloging-in-Publication Data

Hansen, Grace.

 Fruits / Grace Hansen.

   p. cm. -- (Plant anatomy)

ISBN 978-1-68080-136-1 (lib. bdg.)

Includes index.

1. Fruits--Juvenile literature.   I. Title.

575.6/7--dc23

                    2015942104

Table of Contents

Where Fruits Grow

All fruits have seeds. Strawberries have many tiny seeds. Avocados have one big seed!

Fruits grow on trees.
Apples and oranges
grow on trees. Peaches
and pears grow on trees, too.

Fruits also grow on vines and bushes. Grapes grow on vines. Raspberries grow on bushes.

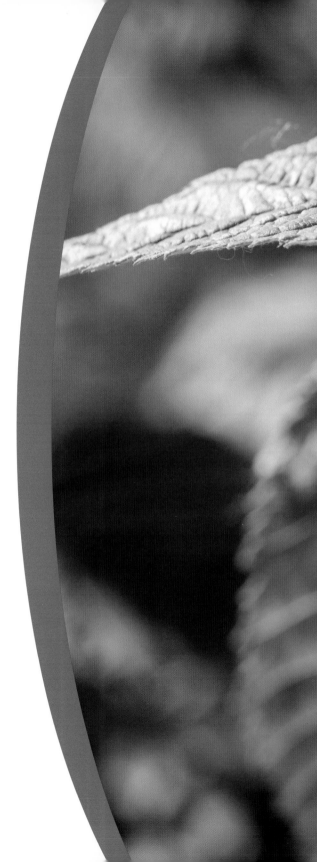

How Fruits Grow

Plants that grow fruits have flowers. Flowers have the parts needed to grow fruit. **Pollination** starts the process.

10

11

Pollen grows on the flower's **anthers**. Pollen has to move to the **stigma**.

12

anther

stigma

13

Insects, wind, and water move pollen. Humans can move pollen, too. The **stigma** is sticky. It catches pollen. The pollen then moves to the **ovary**.

There are **ovules** in the **ovary**. The pollen **fertilizes** the ovules. The ovules grow to become seeds. The ovary grows to become fruit.

bud

flower

seeds

fruit growing
from ovary
of flower

The fruit begins to ripen.

The petals and **sepals** wilt

and fall away. Soon the fruit

will be ready to eat!

Making More Fruits

The fruit can fall to the ground. Wind and water take its seeds far away. The seeds grow into new plants. These plants make more fruit!

Fruit Reproduction

1

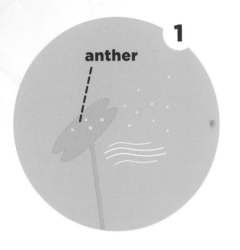

anther

2

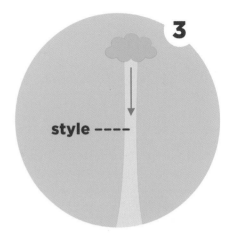

stigma

pollen moves from an anther to a stigma

3

style ----

pollen moves down the style

4

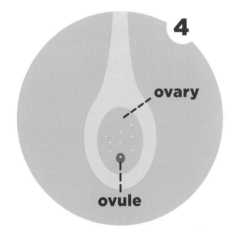

ovary

ovule

pollen enters the ovary and fertilizes an ovule

5

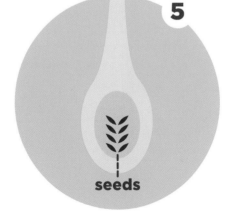

seeds

fertilized ovules become seeds

6

fruit

the ovary grows into a fruit

Glossary

anther – the part of the stamen of a flower that holds pollen.

fertilization – when pollen enters an ovule.

ovary – the large and round bottom part of the pistil that holds the ovules.

ovule – the part of the ovary that after fertilization becomes a seed.

pollination – to give a plant pollen from another plant of the same kind so that seeds can be made.

sepal – one of the leaves that forms to protect a flower bud.

stigma – part of the pistil of a flower which receives pollen grains.

style – part of the pistil of a flower that holds up the stigma.

Index

abdokids.com

Use this code to log on to abdokids.com and access crafts, games, videos, and more!

Abdo Kids Code:
PFK1361